T0193126

THE DECISION THAT CHANGED THE WORLD

ADELEKE DOMINION

authorHOUSE®

AuthorHouse™
1663 Liberty Drive
Bloomington, IN 47403
www.authorhouse.com
Phone: 1 (800) 839-8640

Published by AuthorHouse 04/25/2019

ISBN: 978-1-7283-0420-5 (sc)
ISBN: 978-1-7283-0419-9 (e)

For since by man came death, by Man also came the resurrection of the dead. For as in Adam all die, even so in Christ all shall be made alive.

1 Corinthians 15: 21-22, NKJV

For God so loved the world that He gave His only begotten Son, that whosoever believes in Him should not perish but have everlasting life. For God did not send His Son into the world to condemn the world, but that the world through him might be saved.

John 3:16, NKJV

DECISION

It is important for us to know that our lives will be exactly according to our decisions. If we want a good life, we have to make good decisions. Where we are today is as a result of the decisions we made yesterday. Where we will be tomorrow is as a result of the decisions we make today. Therefore, our lives will be exactly according to our decisions.

Jesus Christ made the decision to die for the sins of humanity. He changed the fabric of the whole world for making this decision. This is because human beings can now have a relationship with their creator. Please, any time you are faced with a decision, make the right decision because your decision will not only affect you but it will affect your families and people around you.

JESUS CHRIST'S DECISION

Jesus Christ is the precious Son of God who came from heaven with the unique purpose of dying for the sins of humanity. He came to reconcile humanity with God through His precious blood. Mary got pregnant through the Holy Spirit and gave birth to Him in a manger. The story of Jesus Christ coming from heaven to the earth to die for the sins of humanity is the greatest love story of all time.

God created Adams for fellowship in the Garden of Eden and God gave him dominion over everything He created. Adam committed sin against God by eating the fruit God told him not to eat. He was given the fruit by his wife. Sins, curses, disaster and every bad things came into the world because of their sins. They also lost dominion which was their inheritance. They also lost the relationship they have with God.

1 Corinthians 15: 21-22, NKJV explain this better: "For since by man came death, by Man also came the resurrection of the dead. For as in Adam all die, even so in Christ all shall be made alive." Through the first Adam, death came into the world but through the second Adam which was Jesus Christ, life and salvation came into this world. Apostle Paul put it this way, "…God was in Christ reconciling the world to Himself, not imputing their trespasses to them, and has committed to us the word of reconciliation" (2 Corinthians 5:19, NKJV).

God has a unique love for humanity. Love without action is nothing but an illusion. God demonstrated His unique love for humanity by sending His only begotten Son to die for their sins (John 3:16, NKJV). This is the time to accept God's love. Who loves you like God? Who protected you all your life? Who gave you life? Who protected your wife? Who protected your husband? Who protected your children? Who protected your family members? It has been Him all the time.

It is crucial for us to know that Jesus Christ

is the precious love offering that God gave to redeem humanity. Jesus Christ came to fulfill the words of the prophets of God. Many prophets prophesied about the birth, ministry, death, and resurrection of Jesus Christ in the Old Testament. Jesus Christ came to fulfill these prophecies in the New Testament. The Old Testament is a shadow but the New Testament is a substance of that shadow. Every event, every revelation, every prophesy and every offering in the Old Testament is a shadow of the life of Jesus Christ in the New Testament. Jesus Christ is a substance of that shadow. From Genesis 1:1 to Revelation 22:21 is the revelations of the precious Lamb of God. History is His story. There is no history without Jesus Christ. There is no life without Jesus Christ. He is the reason for the season. He is the heaven precious Lamb. He is the heaven's special Jewel. His name is better than all the songs they are singing in heaven and on earth. His name is better than all the names in heaven and on earth.

In the Old Testament, the priest would go inside

the temple and killed animals for sacrifice for the sins of the people and his own sins too because he has weaknesses but in the New Testament, Jesus Christ became the sacrificial Lamb that takes away the sins of the world (John 1:29, NKJV). You do not have to live in regret anymore if you accept Jesus Christ as your personal Lord and Savior. You will become a new creature through the precious blood of Jesus Christ (2 Corinthians 5:17, NKJV).

When Jesus Christ was on the cross, blood was gushing out from His head, from His nose, from His lips, from His mouth, from His ear, from His back, from His legs and from every parts of His body. He experienced excruciating pain on the cross. When He was on the cross, your salvation, your healing, your marriage, your aspiration, your peace, your joy, your greatness, your achievement, and your thoughts were on His mind. Jesus Christ went to the cross thinking about you. You are special to Him.

Revelation 5:1-5, 7-13 (NKJV): And I saw in the right hand of Him who sat on the throne a scroll written inside and on the back, sealed with seven seals. Then I saw a strong angel proclaiming with a loud voice, "Who is worthy to open the scroll and to loose its seal? And no one in heaven or on the earth or under the earth was able to open the scroll, or to look at it. So I wept much, because no one was found worthy to open and read the scroll, or look at it. But one of the elders said to me, "Do not weep. Behold, the Lion of the tribe of Judah, the Root of David, has prevailed to open the scroll and to loose its seven seals." Then He came and took the scroll out of the right hand of Him who sat on the throne. Now when He had taken the scroll, the four living creatures and the twenty-four elders fell down before the Lamb, each having a harp, and golden bowls full of incense, which are the prayers of the saints. And they sang a new song, saying: "You are worthy to take the scroll, And to open the seals; For You were slain, And have redeemed us by your blood, Out of every tribe and tongue and people and nation, And have made us kings and priests to our God; And we shall reign on the earth." Then I looked, and I heard the voice of many angels around the throne, the living creatures, and the elders; and the number of them was ten thousand times ten thousand, and thousands of thousands, saying with a loud voice: "Worthy is the Lamb who was slain To receive power and riches and wisdom, And strength and honor and glory and blessing!" And every creature which is in heaven and on the earth and under the earth and such as are in the sea, and all that are in them, I heard saying: "Blessings and honor and glory and power Be to Him who sits on the throne, And to the Lamb, forever and ever!"

All the inhabitants of heaven worshipped God without taking any rest because He is worthy to be praised. They did not have time to go to Burger King to eat ice cream. One day, something strange happened in heaven in which they had to put worship on hold. Everything was on hold.

Why was everything on hold? God asked a unique question through one of His strong angels who was willing to go to the earth and die for the sins of His people. All the angels couldn't do it, the arc angel couldn't do it, the elders couldn't do it. There was silence in heaven for the first time. The salvation of the whole human race was hung up in a balance.

In the decadence of this situation, someone came on the scene and said, "Holy Father, I will die for their sins." Who was this person? This was no other person than the Lamb of God that appeared as if He had been slain from the foundation of the world (Revelation 13:8, NKJV). Jesus Christ of Nazareth was the precious Lamb of God who made the decision to redeem humanity with His blood. Jesus Christ humbled Himself and came all the way from heaven to the earth and died for our sins.

The course of history has forever changed after Jesus Christ made the decision to die for the sins of mankind. This was because God was thinking of destroying the whole human race because of their sins. The soul who sins shall die (Ezekiel 18:20, NKJV). But when Jesus made the decision to die for their sins, God did not have to destroy humanity. Now, we can have a relationship with God through Jesus Christ. Apostle Paul said it better: "...God was in Christ reconciling the world to Himself, not imputing their trespasses to them, and has committed to us the word of reconciliation" (2 Corinthians 5:19, NKJV).

Today is the day of salvation. Do not harden your hearts as you are hearing His voice (Hebrews 3:15, NKJV). If you do not have a relationship with Jesus Christ, today is the day to make a decision to start a relationship with Him. Heaven is real and hell is real too. Please pray this prayer with me: Heavenly Father, I accept the fact that I am a sinner. Right now, I confess my sins before you, and I choose to turn away from my sins. I ask you to cleanse me of all my sins of unrighteousness. I believe that Jesus Christ came into this world and died for my sins and resurrected on the third day. Today, I accept Jesus Christ into my life as my Lord and Savior. Jesus Christ, I will follow you for the rest of my life. I declare I am a born-again child of God in Jesus' name. Amen

If you pray that simple prayer by faith, I believe you have been born again. I encourage you to attend a good church where the Word of God is explained and Jesus Christ is magnified.

CONCLUSION

Please do not let anybody fool you. Your life will be exactly according to your decisions. If you want a good life, please make good decisions. Jesus Christ made the decision to die for the sins of humanity so that human beings can have a relationship with their Heavenly Father. Jesus Christ is the savior of humanity. History is His story. There is no history without Him. He is the heaven precious Lamb who takes away the sins of the world with His precious blood.

PRAYER OF SALVATION

An intimate relationship with God through His Son is the key to a fulfilled and victorious life. If you want to give meaning to your life, your time has come to make the decision to accept Jesus Christ as your personal Lord and Savior. I am going to give you a deal of a life time, and the deal is that this is your time to accept Jesus Christ as your Lord and Savior. Please pray this prayer with me:

Heavenly Father, I accept the fact that I am a sinner. Right now, I confess my sins before you, and I choose to turn away from my sins. I ask you to cleanse me of all my sins of unrighteousness. I believe that Jesus Christ came into this world and died for my sins and resurrected on the third day. Today, I accept Jesus Christ into my life as my Lord and Savior. Jesus Christ, I will follow you for the rest of my life. I declare I am a born-again child of God in Jesus' name. Amen.

If you pray that simple prayer by faith, I believe you have been born again. I encourage you to attend a good church where the Word of God is explained and Jesus Christ is magnified.

ABOUT THE AUTHOR

Adeleke Dominion is a preacher and a motivational speaker. He has been uniquely anointed by God to reveal the mysteries and revelations about God through His Words. He is the founder of Dominion Motivation.

Printed in the United States
By Bookmasters